KAGEROU DAZE 2

C O N T E N T S

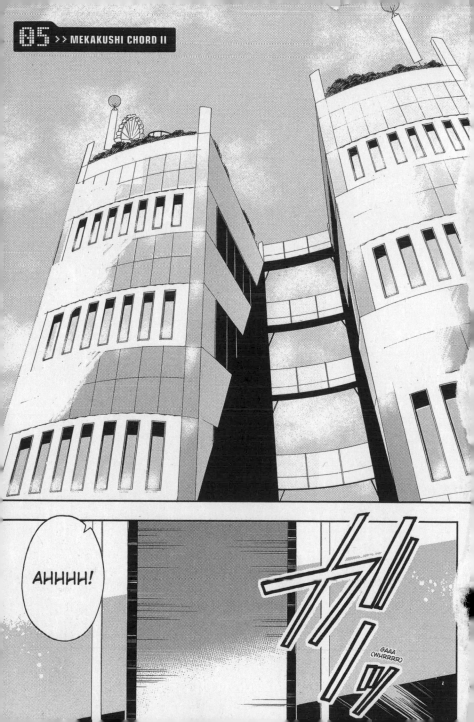

NUH-UH. WE'RE TAKING THE STAIRS, KISARAGI.

HUH? WHY'S THAT?

LET'S SEE... THE PHONES ARE ON THE SEVENTH FLOOR...SO LET'S FIND THE ELEVATOR...

WOW! IT FEELS JUST LOVELY!

NICE AND COOL INSIDE, ISN'T IT?

OH...! WELL, ALL RIGHT, THEN!

WE AREN'T ACTUALLY DISAPPEARING OR ANYTHING, SO...

ENCLOSED PLACES LIKE THAT ARE BAD NEWS.

IF SOMEONE WERE TO *TOUCH* US, MY ABILITY WOULDN'T WORK ANYMORE. EVERYONE WOULD NOTICE YOU.

IS SOMETHING UP? YOU'RE RED AS A BEET.

UH...

HEY, HEY, KISARAGI-CHAN?

YES?

WAS THAT REALLY MY BROTHER BACK THERE? I MUST'VE BEEN SEEING THINGS...

JUST BECAUSE THAT GUY LOOKED EXACTLY LIKE MY BROTHER, IT'S NOT LIKE...

YES! REALLY! I'M JUST FINE!

WELL, IF YOU SAY SO...

YOU SURE? YOU'RE ACTING KINDA WEIRD.

N-NO! NOTH-ING AT ALL!

NO!! NOTH-ING WEIRD AT ALL HERE!!

THIS HAS BEEN A PERFECT DAY, AND THEN THAT BUM HAS TO—

´ACK!

WHATEVER IT IS, YOU'RE DOING A BAD JOB HIDING IT...

NO! I SAW NOTH-ING!!

WOWWW, REALLY? SO WHERE'D YOU SEE HIM, HUH?

LET'S JUST GO.

BUN (FWIP)

NO, NO, NO! WHY DID I SAY THAT!? I'M SO STUPID!!!

UM? YOUR BROTH-ER...?

AAAGH!!! NO! NO, IT'S NOTHING! FORGET ABOUT IT!!!

BUN (WAVE)

BUN

5

WHEEZE!

YEAH...!

I'M ALL RIGHT......

HAFF!

HEY, MARIE-CHAN, ARE YOU OKAY? YOU'RE PRETTY OUT OF BREATH.

NO, I SWEAR, IT'S NOTH-ING!

HEY, MARIE-CHAN!

LET'S BUY SOME NEW TEACUPS LATER, OKAY?

SO...

THE TEACUPS SHE JUST BROKE WERE SOME OF HER FAVORITES, IT SEEMS...

SHE'S REALLY LOOKING FORWARD TO THIS.

OKAY...!

AH...

AHHH!!

DOTEN
(FLUMP)

OBSTACLE-FREE FLOOR

......
GAH!!!

IF SOMEONE WERE TO TOUCH US, MY ABILITY WOULDN'T WORK ANY-MORE...

OH CRAP! HE'S GONNA SEE ME!!

UH... UHHH...

UH, THAT IS...

BA
(VWIP)

NOW WHAT WILL I DO...?

PLEASE, GOD, WHY DID THIS HAVE TO HAPPEN ...!!!?

S-S-SORRY... FOR, UH...

BUN (BOW)

I'M SO SORRY!

UGH... HE SOUNDS SO PATHETIC...

KURU (SPIN)

NO BIG DEAL...

SORRY ABOUT THAT.

...BUT EVEN SO...

HE DIDN'T NOTICE ME HERE...

KIDO-SAN MUST HAVE BEEN FOCUSING ALL OF HER POWER ON US INSTEAD...

WHAT IS THIS PATHETIC CREATURE I SEE BEFORE ME?

HAAA

HEY...

HUH?

KYORO

KYORO (GLANCE)

THAT GUY IS YOUR BROTHER!?

DABA (SWEAT)

ARE YOU FOR REAL, KISARAGI!?

O-OH, MARIE-CHAN! YOU AREN'T HURT, ARE YOU? GOOD.

OH NO, I TORE ONE OF MY NEW SOCKS...

NO WAY, MAN, I DEFINITELY HEARD YOU USE THE WORD "BROTHER" JUST NOW.

I...

NO, HE'S NOT... HE'S NOT... PLEASE...

KANO-SAN, WHY ARE YOU SMIRKING AT ME LIKE THAT? YOU'RE CREEPING ME OUT!

HUH? OH, I DIDN'T MEAN TO... DON'T EVEN WORRY ABOUT IT!

ARRRGH! THIS IS THE AB-SOLUTE WORST !!!

WHY NOW, OF ALL TIMES...!? HE HASN'T MADE ANY ATTEMPT TO LEAVE THE HOUSE IN TWO YEARS!!!

S-SO THAT REALLY IS YOUR BROTHER OVER THERE? REALLY?

UGH...

WHYYY ...!?

HE'S TALKING TO HIS CELL PHONE... HE PROBABLY BROUGHT HER ALONG WITH HIM.

NO! NOT MAD AT ALL! OR CRYING!!!

SURE... ARE YOU MAD, KISA-RAGI?

LOOK, LET'S JUST CARRY ON WITH OUR ERRAND, OKAY? HOW'S THAT SOUND, MARIE-CHAN!!?

KI (GLARE)

PLEASE, BOSS! STOP RE-MINDING ME!!

WH-WHOA...! UH, SORRY...

BIKU (FLINCH)

OKAY, MAYBE NOT THAT MUCH ALIKE. MY BAD.

GUGI (TWITCH)

UUUNH... IT'S JUST SO UNBELIEVABLE... HE JUST HAD TO BE HERE AT THIS EXACT MOMENT, DIDN'T HE...?

HA HA

118

WELL, YOU DO KINDA LOOK ALIKE. LIKE, MAYBE YOU'RE BOTH ON THE SAME WAVELENGTH OR SOME-THING?

HUH?

WE MIGHT HAVE A PROBLEM, THOUGH...

TO THE STAFF, YOU'D BE JUST ANOTHER CUSTOMER THEY WOULDN'T REMEMBER THE NEXT DAY.

PEOPLE WOULD NOTICE YOU AGAIN, BUT YOU STILL WOULDN'T STICK OUT MUCH.

I HAD PLANNED TO INHIBIT MY ABILITY SLIGHTLY SO YOU COULD GET YOUR NEW PHONE.

OH MAN...! BUT MAYBE IF I CAN JUST STAY OUT OF HIS EYE-SIGHT...

I DUNNO... LOOK AT HIM.

BUT IF YOUR BROTHER'S HERE, THAT MAKES THINGS DIFFER-ENT.

YOU'VE SPENT LOTS OF TIME TOGETHER. IF YOU WERE EVEN A LITTLE BIT VISIBLE, HE MIGHT SNIFF YOU RIGHT OUT.

AW, THIS IS SO BOOORING... MAYBE I SHOULD GO HANG OUT WITH YOUR BIG BRO, HUH?

LET'S FIND A MORE DESERTED AISLE.

I DON'T WANT ANY MORE TROU-BLE...

RAAAH, JUST GO AWAY!!

WE'D PROBABLY BETTER WAIT UNTIL HE LEAVES THIS FLOOR, AT LEAST.

KANO-SAN, KNOCK IT OFF...!

KANO... SAN?

SU (SSK)

YEAH... KISARAGI, MARIE, LET'S GET OUT OF HERE.

KIDO, THIS IS BAD.

PIKU (PERK)

GOT IT. YOU TAKE CARE OF THESE GUYS.

TA (DASH)

WHAT NOW? SHOULD WE FALL BACK?

GET KISARAGI'S BROTHER OVER HERE. TRY NOT TO FREAK HIM OUT TOO MUCH.

SURE THING. GET A MOVE ON.

THEIR BACKPACK STINKS OF GUNPOWDER. I CAN SMELL IT FROM HERE.

THEY'RE PROBABLY CARRYING WEAPONS.

UM, BOSS? IS SOMETHING GOING ON...?

THOSE TWO MEN OVER THERE...

HUH...?

DOKUN (BADUM)

16

WH-WHAT...?

KIDO, WHAT'S GOING ON......?

HEY, ONCE KANO COMES BACK, WE'RE LEAVING!

...GH! THIS IS BAD... THAT GUY MUST BE WITH THEM...

DOKUN

DAMMIT... JUST DO EXACTLY AS I SAY, ALL RIGHT?

L-LOOK AT...!

BOSS!

WE'RE PROBABLY IN A—

I DON'T GET WHAT THE BOSS IS TALKING ABOUT...

BUT... WHAT I'M SEEING WITH MY OWN EYES...

DOKUN

DOKUN

PAN

PAN

PAN
(BANG)

PAN

TA
(DASH)

DO
(WHUNK)

GUH...!!

GATA

GATA
(SHIVER)

GATA

GATA

HEY! YOU OKAY?

I-I THINK SO...! ARE YOU ALL RIGHT, MARIE-CHAN!?

CALM DOWN, MARIE! IT'S GONNA BE ALL RIGHT.

THEY HAVEN'T NOTICED US OVER HERE.

ZAWA (MURMUR)
ZAWA
ZAWA

BUT...

THEY'RE WELL-TRAINED AND PROBABLY HAVE EVERY-THING PLANNED OUT.

I CAN ONLY ASSUME THEY INTEND TO TAKE EVERYONE ON THIS FLOOR HOSTAGE...

GREAT... WE'RE PROBABLY DEALING WITH TERRORISTS.

MY BROTHER WAS ON THIS FLOOR.

WHICH MEANS RIGHT NOW HE'S PROBABLY...

FURA
(SWAY)

ONII-CHAN...

HOLD IT!!

WHY IS ALL OF THIS HAPPENING!?

HE MAY BE THAT KIND OF BROTHER, BUT HE'S STILL THE ONLY ONE I HAVE!

......!

KANO WENT OVER THERE TO FIND HIM, REMEMBER?

IF YOU GO TOO, YOU'RE JUST GONNA GET CAUGHT!!

GASHI
(GRAB)

BUT...

BUT IF SOMETHING HAPPENS TO MY BIG BROTHER ...!

PORO
(DRIP)

NO...

THERE'S NO POINT JUMPING IN UNLESS THE SITUATION CHANGES, RIGHT?

THAT THEY'RE TAKING THEM HOSTAGE MEANS THEY AREN'T GOING TO JUST KILL THEM.

KISARAGI! YOU'VE GOT TO STAY CALM FOR ME.

GUSHI

R-RIGHT...

I'M...

SORRY...

GUSHI
(WIPE)

23

SO WHAT ARE WE SUPPOSED TO DO NOW...?

AGH...!

EEP...!

GUUU (VRRRRR)

BIKU (FLINCH)

OH MAN... IF THIS KEEPS UP, WE'LL ALL...

IT MUST BE THE POLICE.

I CAN HEAR VOICES FROM THE OTHER SIDE OF THE SHUTTERS.

A...A TEXT?

WHA...?

GOSO (RSTL)

SU (FWIP)

TCH...

UM...SO WHO'S IT FROM?

......HUH?

KYOTON (STUNNED)

とん.

AH!

...FROM THAT IDIOT...

PASHI (SNATCH)

POI (TOSS)

...HOW IS HE TYPING ON HIS CELL PHONE IF HE'S BEEN CAUGHT?

THE TERRORISTS MUST'VE THOUGHT HE WAS TOO BIG AN IDIOT TO WASTE THE TAPE ON BINDING HIS HANDS.

IS HE... IS HE IN TROUBLE?

UH, K-KIDO...?

PRETTY MUCH. HE'S BEYOND HELP...

BOSS, IS...IS SOMETHING WRONG WITH HIS HEAD, OR...?

TROUBLE? HE'S MENTALLY UNSTABLE.

I NEED TO TAKE HIM TO A DOCTOR FOR A LOBOTOMY.

BUT KANO'S HAVING SO MUCH FUN!

I THINK...

...THIS IS STILL A PRETTY BAD SITUATION...

SO, UH... BOSS...?

......

BUT...

THIS IS GETTING SO SILLY.

WHAT...?

KANO'S BOUND UP WITH THE REST. OR AT LEAST, IT LOOKS THAT WAY TO EVERYONE ELSE.

...REALLY, THOUGH. WHY ISN'T HE TIED UP?

STUPID OR NOT, THEY'D STILL TIE HIM UP.

WHAT DO YOU MEAN...?

WAIT... WHAT...?

HYOKO (ZOOP)

OOH, SO HE'S DISGUISED HIMSELF AGAIN?

BASICALLY, HE HAS WHAT WE CALL "DECEIVING EYES."

IF MY ABILITY IS TO GO "INVISI-BLE"...

...THEN HIS IS TO "APPEAR DIFFERENTLY" FROM WHAT HE ACTUALLY IS.

ACK!

THAT'S SUCH A CUTE EXAMPLE, KIDO!

AW!

IMAGINE YOU FOUND A KITTEN ON THE STREET. BUT YOU TAKE IT HOME AND—WHOOPS! IT'S ACTUALLY A ROTTWEILER. IT'S KIND OF LIKE THAT.

BUT... HOW DOES THAT EVEN...?

SO HE CAN MAKE... OPTICAL ILLUSIONS...?

W-WE'RE NOT GETTING ANY PETS...

NO, I... QUIT IT, MARIE.

HUH?

BUT IT DOESN'T HAVE MUCH RANGE. HE CAN ONLY DO IT ON HIMSELF.

YEAH, THAT'S CLOSE ENOUGH.

BUT... DID HE NOT WANT US TO NOTICE, OR...?

WOW... HE LOOKED LIKE HE WAS JUST WALKING ALONG WITH US...

REMEMBER OUR WALK HERE? HE DIDN'T LOOK IT, BUT HE WAS ACTUALLY RUNNING LOOKOUT THE WHOLE TIME.

KANO-SAN... GRINNING EAR TO EAR LIKE THAT MAKES YOU LOOK SO STUPID...

YEAH...

HE'S A TOTAL IDIOT...

...STILL, THOUGH...

BUT THEN AGAIN...

HIS SILLY ANTICS HAVE HELPED MARIE-CHAN AND ME CALM DOWN, I GUESS...

MAYBE HE'S ACTUALLY PRETTY CAPABLE.

HMM?

I GUESS HE'S EVEN MORE UNLUCKY THAN I AM.

FOR THIS TO BE THE FIRST THING HE SEES AFTER TWO YEARS IN HIS ROOM...

AND MEAN- WHILE... ALL MY BROTHER DOES IS MAKE ME WORRY!

Well—

Afternoon, coppers. Thanks for coming.

BIKU (FLINCH)

HM? SURE, BUT...

CAN I BORROW YOUR PHONE? I WANT TO BRAINSTORM IN TEXT A LITTLE MORE.

......WHAT DO YOU MEAN?

I'm only gonna say this once, so pay attention.

Basically, we have just one demand—

IS THAT THE TERRORISTS? WHAT DO THEY...?

GOKURI (GULP)

UH, WELL... IT'S KIND OF HARD TO PUT INTO WORDS...

The hand-off...

WELL, PFFT.

We want one billion yen within thirty minutes.

...UH, HANG ON.

WHO'S THIS WEIRD GIRL YOU HAVE SHOWING UP MID-WAY!?

WELL, IT'S JUST LIKE IT'S WRITTEN DOWN, SO...

UH, IT'S SOMEONE I KNOW, AND...

OOH, THAT'S MY NAME AT THE END!!

MM-HMM, HMM...

HUH...

THIS IS THE BEST PLAN I CAN THINK OF RIGHT NOW...

SHE WILL...OR SHOULD... PROBABLY...

B-BUT THAT'S WHAT I WANT KANO-SAN TO CHECK ON!

AND SHE'LL ACTUALLY DO THAT...?

...ASSUMING SHE'S ACTUALLY THERE, THEN MAYBE...

HUH?

SO IS IT ALL RIGHT IF I TEXT THIS TO HIM...?

......

HEY, UM... SO WHAT ARE WE DOING...?

HERE, UH... LET ME SEND THIS...!

O-OKAY!

GOT IT!

I'LL TRY TO BE READY!!

GU
(CLENCH)

OH, MARIE-CHAN... WELL, UH...

I'LL GIVE YOU A SIGNAL! SO JUST STICK CLOSE UNTIL THEN!

...?

NO...

...BUT THIS IS GOING TO WORK...

I'M NOT TOTALLY CONFIDENT ABOUT A LOT OF THIS...

KANO-SAN JUST REPLIED......

VUU
(VRRR)

WE'RE GONNA HAVE TO MAKE IT WORK!

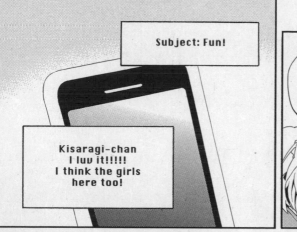

Subject: Fun!

Kisaragi-chan I luv it!!!!! I think the girls here too!

UMM...

WHAT'D HE SAY?

Everythings ok here, I got a few more shots of—

DELETE THIS TEXT?

YES NO

PON (CLICK)

I know cuz I hear her voice talkin and I think I luv her! Shes a keeper!!

WHEW...

Ill check for sure but can u get closer w/o gettin caught?

ZA

YOU THINK WE'LL BE SAFE IF WE TRY GETTING CLOSER?

SURE, IF WE DON'T BUMP INTO ANY-ONE.

BUT—

ZA (SKFF)

YEAH? GOOD.

I THINK IT'S ALL GOOD ON HIS END.

TU

5U (FWP)

YOU OKAY, MARIE-CHAN? NOT SCARED OR ANYTHING?

NOPE!

I WANNA BEAT THESE BAD GUYS TOO!!

WE CAN'T LET THEM DO THIS TO US...

WE CAME HERE TO GO SHOPPING, AFTER ALL.

I HAVE TO SEE THIS WHOLE OPERATION THROUGH!!!

I'M FINALLY JUST ABOUT TO MAKE SOME REAL FRIENDS HERE...

SHE'S RIGHT.

MARIE-CHAN...

AH.

THERE'S YOUR BROTHER, KISARAGI...

AND THAT IDIOT.

OH!

...MARIE, WHAT'RE YOU DOING?

HM. GUESS YOU REALLY ARE SIBLINGS, HUH?

HE'S USUALLY A MASSIVE WIMP, BUT HE LOOKS SO CONFIDENT NOW... I HAVE A FEELING HE'S THINKING THE SAME THING I AM.

LOOK AT MY BROTHER... ALL SERIOUS LIKE THAT...

AND STOP GRINNING.

AT LEAST TRY TO HIDE A LITTLE, DUMBASS...

UH, I THOUGHT THIS LOOKED REALLY NEAT, SO...!

BIYAAAAN (WHIRRRRR)

SURE! I'LL PUT IT RIGHT BACK!

...YEAH, GREAT. PUT IT BACK LATER, OKAY...?

A HANDHELD MASSAGER...?

KOKU (NOD)

AH...

AAAAAGH!!!!

GOCHIIIN
(CRAAACK)

NGH!?

TA
(DASH)

WHO...

KUH!

BA
(SNATCH)

PANT! HFF! HAFF! WHEEZE!

YOU...

WHOA, WAIT... I DIDN'T DO IT...

URGH!

DOKA (WHACK)

HUH !!!?

WHO THE HELL YOU THINK YOU'RE PUNCHING IN THE HEAD!!?

BOGU (SLAM)

I THOUGHT FOR SURE WE WERE DEAD... IS THIS REALLY GONNA WORK?

KUA (SNARL)

ARE YOU STUPID!? DO YOU WANT TO GET US KILLED!?

HAAH....

I-I'M SORRY...!!

EEP...!

BIKU (FLINCH)

I think were good~

Your bro just said 100% sure of takedown if he get a chance!!!!

Some dude huh!? O and lololol guyzzz that was sweeeet!!!

OH... IT'S KANO-SAN...

VUU (VRRR)

VUU

ALL RIGHT... I'M READY...!

MARIE, STAY WITH ME UNTIL I SAY IT'S OKAY, ALL RIGHT?

LET'S KEEP THIS OPERATION GOING!

UH? OH!

ALL RIGHT...!

This is startin to be boring... wanna go home...

O I told ur bro to wait til beerd dude starts talkin again so

I THINK IT'S ALL GOOD OVER THERE.

WE'RE THE ONLY ONES WHO CAN DO THIS!

BUT I THINK WE CAN DO THIS...

NO...

WE WON'T HAVE A VERY BIG WINDOW...

WHAT !?

I'm taking ten minutes off the deadline for the money.

Hey... You guys hearing me?

ZAWA (KRIZZT)

...!!

YOU CAN'T GO RUNNING IN BY YOURSELF!

YOU'RE THE ONLY ONE WHO KNOWS HOW WE'RE TIMING THIS THING!

SHE'S RIGHT, BUT......

I DON'T REALLY GET IT...

...BUT IT'S ALL RIGHT.

HUH...?

SU (SSK)

BUT MY BROTHER ......!

GU (SQUEEZE)

KI...

KISA-RAGI!

MY EYES FEEL SO WARM.

NOW...

...I CAN SEE EVERY- THING.

AND THEY'RE LOCATED...

BOSS!!

UH, OKAY...!

MARIE, LET'S GO.

GOT IT.

WE'LL START WITH THAT!

THE 42-INCH TV, THIRD FROM THE LEFT!

DA
(DASH)

MY BROTHER'S USUALLY SUCH AN UNRELIABLE WUSS, BUT JUST NOW, HE SEEMED KINDA COOL, HUH.

ALL RIGHT!

NOW!

NOW THAT EVERY-ONE'S FOCUSED ON HIM...

IN THIS MOMENT...

CHARGE!

...NH!?

BA
(CRUSH)

...BUT I DIDN'T WANT THE TERRORISTS TO START FIRING AT THE COPS.

YEAH, I FIGURED MY BROTHER WOULD GET THE SHUTTER OPEN FOR US...

LIKE, GETTING EVERYONE TO FOCUS ON MARIE LIKE THAT.

THAT WAS SOME PRETTY IMPRESSIVE QUICK THINKING, YOU KNOW?

ZURU (DRAG)

ZURU

...AND THEN I REMEMBERED KANO-SAN GETTING PETRIFIED, SO...

SO I WAS TRYING TO FIGURE OUT HOW TO KEEP EVERYONE WHERE THEY WERE...

DELETED 'EM.

OH, DID YOU SEE THE PICS I SENT, KIDO?

HEY, MAN, QUIT BEING MEAN!

HUH...... SO THAT DUMBASS ACTUALLY CAME IN HANDY.

AC Ne

AWW!

KON

KA

YEP.

...GUESS THAT'S IT... ISN'T IT?

WELL...

KETA (TRMBL)

PFFT... HA HA HA...!

OF ALL THE WEAPONS TO PICK! SHE'S A COMEDIC GENIUS, MAN!

OH MAN... MY GUT...

THAT'S THE MASSAGER SHE WHAPPED THAT STUBBLE-BEARD GUY WITH!

THAT STUPID...! SHE WENT TO PUT THAT THING BACK!

OH MAN... HE'S BAR-RAGING HER WITH QUES-TIONS...

NOW WHAT!? THIS IS PRETTY BAD, ISN'T IT!?

WARA (CROWD)

WARA (CROWD)

WARA

OH GREAT, NOW THERE'S MORE OF THEM...

DAM-MIT... NOW WHAT ...?

WE HAVE TO GET HER BACK HERE FAST...

DOSA (WHUMP)

WILL YOU SHUT UP FOR A MINUTE!!?

GNGH !!

BOGUN (WHAP)

SA (SHWP)

LET'S...

LET'S...

OH NO... KIDO'S "CONCEALING" HAS BEEN REMOVED... HE'S BEEN EXPOSED!

DO (THUMP)

AAAGH!!?

WHERE DID YOU COME FROM...!?

GUI (GRAB)

MARIE-CHAN!

DA (DASH)

RUN!!

GET OUTTA HERE!!

IF THEY ONLY LOOKED AWAY FOR A MOMENT...

...I COULD CONCEAL YOU...

BOSS, YOU TAKE MARIE-CHAN'S HAND FOR ME..!

WAIT! WHERE ARE YOU GOING!!?

TA (TMP) TA TA

BA (BLINK)

HUH!?

ZAWA (CLAMOR)

!!?

ZAWA
ZAWA (MURMUR)

THE FREEZING'S WORN OFF!!

KANO! HEY! PICK UP KISARAGI'S BROTHER AND GET MOVING!

WHAAA? MAN, WHAT A PAIN IN THE...

AH!

HEY......

THEY'RE... GONE...?

OH! RIGHT!

NNNGH... GIMME A BREAK, MAAAN...

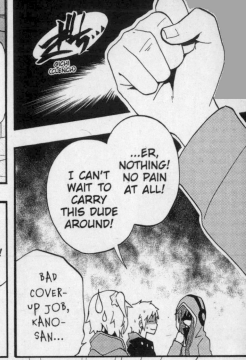

GICHI (CLENCH)

...ER, NOTHING! NO PAIN AT ALL!

I CAN'T WAIT TO CARRY THIS DUDE AROUND!

BAD COVER-UP JOB, KANO-SAN...

HEY! ENE-CHAN! YOU THERE?

WHAT HAPPENED TO MY MASTER!?

WOW! ARE YOU OUT SHOPPING TOO!?

OHH! IS THAT YOU, MOMO-SAN!!?

UHH... I'LL EXPLAIN LATER, OKAY?

YOU MIND COMING WITH US?

NO NEW PHONE, NO NEW TEACUPS... WE DIDN'T ACCOMPLISH A THING.

AHH...... WHAT ON EARTH DID I EVEN COME HERE FOR...?

C'MON! WE'RE GOING!!

UH... NO, NOT EXACTLY...

OH, TO THE AMUSE- MENT PARK!?

O-OKAY!!

THOUGH...

!

I MEAN, MOMO-CHAN?

Y-YEAH, KISA—

...IF I CAN BE SAID TO HAVE ACCOM-PLISHED ANYTHING HERE...

HEY, MARIE-CHAN?

KAGEROU
DAZE

KAGEROU
DAZE

SHINTARO KISARAGI. AGE: 18. JOB: SHUT-IN.

HOBBIES: MESSING AROUND WITH COMPUTERS.

AND NOW I FIND MYSELF IN THIS STRANGE BUILDING WITH NO IDEA OF WHERE I AM.

MY SISTER, MOMO, IS HERE WITH ME FOR SOME REASON...

—OH, RIGHT!

...AND SHE JUST FILLED ME IN ON THE EVENTS THAT LED US **BOTH** HERE.

SO... THANKS FOR SAVING ME, I GUESS...?

UNGH...

SOMETHIN' TELLS ME HE REALLY WANTS TO SAY SOMETHIN' ELSE......

I HAVE NO IDEA WHAT'S GOING ON......

GYU
(CLENCH)

I'D REALLY BETTER NOT GET INVOLVED WITH THESE—

WELL, MAN, I'M SURE YOU'VE GOT A TON OF QUESTIONS FOR US!

UH...?

THIS GOES WAY BEYOND QUIRKY...

AN INVISIBLE WOMAN, A MEDUSA, THIS CHAMELEON GUY...

THIS IS A SERIOUSLY DANGEROUS GANG!!

DON'T WORRY ABOUT IT. WE'RE HAPPY TO BE OF SERVICE!

LEMME JUST INTRODUCE US AGAIN...

KANO.

SO YOU DON'T HAFTA BE NERVOUS AT ALL OR ANY—

YUP!

WHAT'S WITH THOSE STUPID MEMBER-SHIP NUMBERS?

AND WHAT'S HE MEAN, "FREAKY" ...?

HUH... I SEE...

WISE, THERE'S TIME,

...READ DOWN IN HERE, ONCE YOU GET USED TO EVERY-THING!

SHINTARO-KUN...

W-WAIT!

GIVE ME A SEC-OND!

ISN'T THIS THE SAME SITUATION MOMO TOLD ME ABOUT...?

OH MAN, THIS ISN'T GOOD...

BOGU (WHAM)

OH NO, DID I...?

AH!

YOU DID IT AGAIN...

YEOW!

......

I KNEW THIS WOULD HAPPEN!!

GO

GO

GO

GO (RMBL)

I GUESS NOW THAT YOU KNOW OUR SECRETS, WE CAN'T LET YOU GO...

...HUH? HOW OLD AM I? OH, DON'T TELL ME YOU FORGOT, MOM!

THEY MADE ME MEMBER NO. 7!

I JOINED THIS THING CALLED THE MEKAKUSHI-DAN!

I JUST MADE SOME NEW FRIENDS!

AWW... WELL, IT'S A BIT FAR, BUT THERE'S ANOTHER ONE IN THE SUBURBS!

I BET IT'S CLOSED TODAY, AFTER ALL THE STUFF THAT HAPPENED.

OH, UH, BUT PROBABLY NOT THE DEPART-MENT STORE ONE.

MASTER! GET UP SO WE CAN GO TO THE AMUSEMENT PARK!

I'M EIGH-TEEN YEARS OLD ...!!

SHINTARO.

WISH I COULDA SEEN YOU SOAKED IN TEA!

NOW I CAN GO OUT WITHOUT HAVING TO WORRY ABOUT A THING!

I'M JUST GLAD MY PHONE'S WORKING AGAIN.

ENE-CHAN TOLD ME, YOU KNOW! SHE SAID, "MY MASTER'S SEXUAL DRIVE IS LIMIT-LESS"!

THAT'S REALLY EMBAR-RASSING TO ME, YOU KNOW!!?

YOU'RE HORRI-BLE!! I CAN'T BELIEVE YOU!!

YOU'RE JUST LOOKING AT DIRTY PICS THE WHOLE TIME YOU'RE IN YOUR ROOM!

WHAT ABOUT YOUR HABITS, HUH!?

THE SAME MISTAKE MULTIPLE TIMES A DAY......?

UH...

WHOA, WHOA, THIS AIN'T GOOD.

...YOU HAVE TO RUN OUT OF THE ROOM EACH TIME YOU CLICK ON THAT PAGE TOO...

ENE-CHAN TOLD ME...

!!

EVERYONE MAKES MISTAKES, YOU KNOW!?

OH REALLY?

OH RIGHT... THAT. I JUST ACCIDENTALLY CLICKED ON SOME WEIRD BANNER AD, OKAY!?

I SAID, YOU LOOK GROSS!

HELLO? ARE YOU LISTEN-ING!?

SHE USED TO BE A LOT CUTER... CALLING ME "ONII-CHAN, ONII-CHAN" AND ALL THAT...

. . . .

THAT OUTFIT IS SO LAME TOO.

THIS ISN'T SOME KIND OF SWEATING CONTEST, YOU KNOW.

SO WHAT?

I'M NOT CAUSING YOU ANY PROBLEMS.

UH...

WHAT!?

DID THEY MAKE YOU WEAR THAT AFTER LOSING A BET, OR WHAT?

AND BESIDES, WHAT ABOUT YOUR OUTFIT, HUH?

鎖

大江戸

国

MOMO GRAY SHIRT: ISOLATED
WHITE SHIRT: GREATER EDO

PFFT!

YOU SPEND TOO MUCH TIME INDOORS— THAT'S WHY YOU GET TOO EXHAUSTED TO WALK.

BUT YOU CAN'T DO THIS FOREVER, Y'KNOW, MARIE.

SHUT-IN FOR TWO YEARS

I-I KNOW... I'LL TRY TO GO ON LONGER WALKS...

...AND NOW ALL THIS SQUABBLING ABOUT A STUPID NAME...?

FIRST I'M FORCED OUT-DOORS...

..."SETTO" IS KINDA COOL TOO, MAYBE...

BUT...

HAH.

IN FACT, MARIE'S REALLY EASY. SHE'S SO LIGHT!

HM? OH, I'M FINE. I CARRY AROUND ALL KINDS OF STUFF IN MY LINE OF WORK, SO IT'S NORMAL FOR ME.

I GOTTA SAY......I'M IMPRESSED YOU CAN CARRY SOMEONE IN THIS HEAT.

KIRA (SPARKLE)

SAY... WHERE DID KIDO GO, ANY-WAY?

HER AND THAT KANO GUY TOO...

THEY SAID THEY'D JOIN US LATER!

WELL, KIDO'S SKILL DOESN'T WORK IF YOU BUMP INTO FOLKS...

IT'S REALLY NO PROBLEM! BESIDES, I LIKE WALKING!

I'M REALLY SORRY FOR THIS, GUYS.

I WISH WE COULD'VE TAKEN THE BUS...

鎖　国

SORRY TO KEEP YOU.

NOT AT ALL! WE ONLY JUST GOT HERE!

RIGHT!

THAT'S EXACTLY IT!

NI CGRIND

I WANNA GO ON THE ROLLER COASTER!!!

I HAVEN'T BEEN TO AN AMUSEMENT PARK IN AGES!

WHAT SHOULD WE RIDE FIRST, HUH?

WHEE!

YAY!

......I...

I'D BETTER CALL THEM!

WOW, LOOK AT ALL THE PEOPLE GETTING OFF...

IS THAT THE BOSS?

OHH, IT IS!!

OKAY!

WE'LL BE WAITING RIGHT HERE, ALL RIGHT?

UH, HELLO, BOSS? YOU THERE?

WE'RE RIGHT BY THE GATE...

SO AS LONG AS WE'VE GOT KIDO'S ABILITY...

...YOU CAN ENJOY THE PARK ALL YOU WANT TO... RIGHT?

THOSE SNAKING RAILS...

TWISTING OVER AND OVER THEMSELVES IN DYNAMIC HORROR...

AND THE WHEELS OF DISASTER FLYING OVER THEM...

YOU CALL THEM "CARS." I CALL THEM "COFFINS."

OKAY!

BETTER TIE BACK YOUR HAIR, MARIE. IT MIGHT GET CAUGHT IN SOMETHING.

NO PROBLEM HERE...

YOU ALL RIGHT, KIDO?

WHOO! FIRST ROW!!

WHY DO I HAVE TO BE HERE.........?

I...

OH, OF COURSE HE IS. HE'S MY BROTHER!

I...

YOU STILL WITH US TOO, SHINTARO-KUN?

108

AAAAAAA

GOTON
(CLUNK)

WHOO-HOO!!

KATA
(CLACKA)

KATA

KATA

KATAN
(CLANK)

KATA

KATA

KATAN

KATA

RRH...
BLRRH...

UH,
ONII......?

WAS
IT?

YOU SEE?
THAT
WASN'T
SO BAD!

WHEW!
THAT
WAS A
TOTAL
BLAST!

THAT SURE WAS A SURPRISE, MAN, YOU TOSSIN' IT OUT OF THE BLUE.

FEELING BETTER YET, SHINTARO-KUN?

YEAH...

SORRY...

DONYORI (GLOOM)

09 >> HEADPHONE ACTOR I

KUA (YAWN)

...ALL THESE GUYS ARE YOUNGER THAN ME...

MOMO MENTIONED...

I MEAN, HOW CHILDISH ARE THESE GUYS ANYWAY...?

REALLY, THOUGH... AN AMUSEMENT PARK...?

...THIS IS MORE THAN JUST SOME CLIQUE FOR WEIRD KIDS.

...NOT TO MENTION THOSE WACKY ABILITIES THEY HAVE...

BUT JUDGING BY HOW THEY DISPATCHED THOSE TERRORISTS YESTERDAY...

...BUT NOW IT'S GOT SEVEN MEMBERS, COUNTING ME.

APPARENTLY IT WAS ONLY KIDO, SETO, AND KANO AT FIRST...

WHAT WAS THIS GROUP EVEN CREATED FOR IN THE FIRST PLACE?

...THE WEIRDEST THING IS HOW MUCH THEY SEEM TO KNOW...

...ABOUT ALL THE ABILITIES THEY HAVE.

AND EXCEPT FOR ME, THEY ALL HAVE... SOME KIND OF ABILITY TOO.

BUT...

114

...SPEAKING OF...

...WHADDAYA THINK ABOUT KISARAGI-CHAN, SETO?

NI (GRIN)

YOU'RE USUALLY BUSY WITH WORK ALL DAY, SETO.

YEAH. AND IT'S REALLY THE FIRST TIME TOO WHEN YOU THINK ABOUT IT.

IT'S NICE, THOUGH, ISN'T IT? ALL OF US HAVING FUN TOGETHER!

HA HA HA!

YEAH, NO KIDDING. BUT, LIKE, THE MORE THE MERRIER, RIGHT?

...BUT SEEIN' A WHOLE MESS OF NEW FACES WHEN I GOT BACK YESTERDAY! WOW!

YEAH, TRUE...

TOTALLY FRAZZLED, LEMME TELL YOU... HEE-HEE!

YOU SHOULD'VE SEEN KIDO WHEN SHE BROUGHT HER IN FOR THE FIRST TIME.

AND, I MEAN, WOW, A REAL POP IDOL!

OH, SHE'S GREAT! REAL POLITE TOO.

PIKU (TWITCH)

BUT WHAT'S, LIKE, MOTIVATING HER, D'YOU THINK? IS SHE BEING CONTROLLED BY SOMEONE?

OH, AND ENE-CHAN TOO!

TALK ABOUT ONE CRAZY CHARACTER, HUH?

OF COURSE NOT!

ONE OF THOSE, YOU KNOW, "CASUAL ENCOUNTERS" SITES, OR...?

YEAH, HOW'D YOU COME TO KNOW THAT GIRL IN THE FIRST PLACE, HUH!?

PIKU (TWITCH)

PIKU

I DON'T KNOW WHO SHE IS... OR WHERE SHE CAME FROM.

SHE'S JUST BEEN LIVING IN MY COMPUTER FOR A WHILE NOW...

SHE WON'T TELL ME ANYTHING.

HMM, YES... YES...

I SEE...

SO IT'S LIKE...

ENE'S PAST, HUH...?

I MEAN...

...YOU KEPT PESTERING ENE-CHAN ABOUT HER PAST "ENCOUNTERS"...

...AND THEN SHE GOT PISSED ABOUT IT...?

NO! WHAT'RE YOU EVEN ASKING ME!?

I DON'T REMEMBER EVER SAYING ANYTHING LIKE THAT!

ANYWAY, SHINTARO-SAN!

GOTTA ENJOY YOURSELF WHILE YOU'RE HERE, RIGHT?

BISHI (POINT)

...I DON'T REALLY CARE ABOUT HER PAST.

IF SHE DOESN'T WANNA TALK ABOUT IT...

HEY, HEY!

LET'S NOT FIGHT ABOUT IT!

SU (ZWIP)

HOW 'BOUT THIS!!?

118

SUKKU
(SHOOOP)

BIKU

THIS IS IT!!!

...THIS IS MY CHANCE TO SPREAD MY WINGS BY MYSELF ...!!

BIKU (STARTLE)

SEE YA!!!

ALONE! BY MYSELF! YOU FOLLOW ME?

I JUST THOUGHT I'D WANDER AROUND A BIT!!

KOFF!

HEART ATTACK?

WHOA, MAN... WHAT'S GOTTEN INTO YOU ALL OF A SUDDEN ...?

WHAT? NO!

THAT IS...

WHEN DID I LAST HAVE PRIVATE TIME LIKE THIS?

I DID IT...

SUTA

SUTA

SUTA

SUTA

SUTA (STRIDE)

SAWAAAAA
(BLISSSS)

JUST LOOK AT HOW FREE I AM NOW!!!

IF I'M ASLEEP, SHE JARS ME AWAKE. IF I'M ON THE NET, SHE SABOTAGES ME...

I'VE LIVED IN CONSTANT FEAR OF ENE, DAY AND NIGHT.

HEY...

BUT NOW LOOK AT ME!!

I'VE BEEN FREED FROM HER EVIL CURSE!

HELLO?

CAN YOU HEAR ME, SHINTARO...?

WHOOO!!! BEING ALONE IS AWE-SOOOME!!!!

BA
(FWOOP)

SINCE WHEN HAS SHE BEEN BEHIND ME...!?

UMM...

AHHH, SORRY, SORRY!

HUH? AH!

...WHY ARE YOU IGNORING ME......?

GUZU (SNIFF)

UMM... HEY!

MARIE!!

DON'T CRY, OKAY?

OKAY!?

THE GREAT ICE LABYRINTH

SO, WHAT IS IT? IS SOMETHING WRONG?

KOKUN (NOD)

SU (SHP)

SEE YA.

WHY DON'T YOU ASK SOMEONE ELSE?

AH...

OH GREAT. IF I SAY NO AFTER SHE'S GOTTEN HERSELF ALL WORKED UP...

YES! IT'S COUPLES ONLY...

THAT? WHAT ABOUT THAT? ...DID YOU WANT TO GO IN?

KOKU KOKU (NOD)

ZAWA (MURMUR)

SECURITY!

GET THAT MAN......!!

WAAAAAH!!!

OKAY...

DUMB SHUT-IN!!

YOU DROP-OUT!!

JOB-LESS!!!

FRIGGIN' VIRGIN!!!

THAT STRANGE MAN JUST ATTACKED AN INNOCENT GIRL!!!

WE'LL TAKE CARE OF HIM, MA'AM!!!!

HA

DA (DASH)

YEAH! I WANNA GO IN! SO COME WITH ME!!

WOULD THAT MAKE YOU HAPPY?

...ALL RIGHT, MARIE.

DON (BOOM)

WHERE'S EVERYONE ELSE, MARIE?

WAIT...? ALL THE GIRLS SHOULD BE TOGETHER...

DID SHE CIRCLE ALL THE ATTRACTIONS SHE WANTS TO VISIT...!?

UH... SURE...

...SO WE GOT SEPA-RATED.

BUT I GOT IN THE WRONG LINE...

WELLLL KIDO, MOMO-CHAN, AND I WENT TO GO ON THE ROLLER COASTER AGAIN...

MOKU

MOKU

MOKU

MOKU

MOKU (SCRITCH)

124

C'MON, LET'S GO! THE LINE'S REALLY SHORT TOO!

MARIE'S A LOT MORE PROACTIVE THAN I THOUGHT!

WELL, MOMO'S SAFE WITH KIDO, I GUESS...

OH, I SEE.

BETTER NOT KEEP 'EM WAITING. YOU CAN PUT THE CAP BACK ON INSIDE, MARIE...

OH, WE'RE UP ALREADY...

NEXT COUPLE, PLEASE!

A-ALL RIGHT...!

HUH? SURE, I GUESS...

A LITTLE TEA WOULDN'T HURT.

WE'D BETTER DRINK SOME TEA RIGHT NOW, JUST IN CASE, RIGHT...!?

THIS IS GONNA BE A BIG LABYRINTH, RIGHT, SHINTARO?

KAPO (POP)

HYOOOO (WHOOSH)

WHOA...

PRETTY CHILLY IN HERE, HUH...?

GACHI
GACHI
GACHI (SHIVER)

...IT-T-T'S... IT... C-C-COLD-D-D... I'M G-G-GONNA D-D-D-DIIIIIE...!!!

...WHAT DID YOU EVEN COME IN HERE FOR...?

I KNOW HOW HOT YOU GET ALL THE TIME, MARIE...

IT MUST FEEL—

O-OKAY. TH-TH-THANK...

AH...

HERE, LET ME HAVE THAT BOTTLE. YOU DON'T WANNA DROP IT IN HERE.

OH COME ON, YOU AREN'T GONNA FREEZE TO DEATH!

I...I-I DIDN'T TH-TH-THINK IT'D BE THIS C-C-COLD...

BISHAAAAAAAA (SPLAAAAASH)

ACHOO!!

TSURUN (SLIP)

126

SO, TO RECAP...

HAUNTED GROTESQUE DOLLHOUSE

YEAH, BUT SHE'S KIND OF IN TROUBLE RIGHT NOW...!

HEY... WEREN'T YOU WITH MOMO...?

GUI (SPIN)

THEN, ON ACCOUNT OF OTHER *"CIRCUM-STANCES,"* YOU CAN'T GO BACK IN ALONE.

BUT DUE TO *"CIRCUM-STANCES,"* AS YOU PUT IT, YOU LEFT BY YOURSELF.

YOU AND MOMO WENT INTO THE HAUNTED HOUSE TOGETHER.

I'M GLAD I CAN COUNT ON YOU. YOU'RE SO QUICK ON THE UPTAKE...

Y-YES! RIGHT!

...SHE'S STUCK IN THERE BY HERSELF. IS THAT IT?

AND SINCE SHE'LL ATTRACT CROWDS IF YOU AREN'T AROUND...

YOU'RE SCARED WITLESS, HUH...

MAN, THOUGH...

BUTSU BUTSU BUTSU BUTSU BUTSU (MUTTER)

...THIS IS A PRETTY FANCY-LOOKING HAUNTED HOUSE!

WELL...

ISN'T IT, KI—

KURU (SPIN)

...SO SHE SEARCHED FOR SOMEONE TO JOIN HER...?

SHE'S TOO SCARED TO GO BACK IN BY HERSELF...

I'M NOT SCARED OF SOME STUPID KIDDIE ATTRACTION...!

NO, I'M NOT!!

SHAKA (TING)

SHAKA

SHAKA

SHAKA

PURU
PURU (TRMBL)
PURU

I-I KNOW THAT... BUT...!!

SHE'S ACTING LIKE A NEW-BORN GOAT...

PURU
PURU
PURU
PURU

BAI CYANO

HOW ARE WE SUPPOSED TO FIND MOMO IF I CAN'T EVEN TALK TO YOU!?

YOU DUMB-ASS!

WHAT ARE YOU DOING, SHIN-TARO !!!?

AAAGH !!!

UH, HEY...

KIDO...?

SUTA SUTA SUTA SUTA (STRIDE) SUTA SUTA SUTA SUTA

AH!

SO (PEEK)

THAT ISN'T...

UNH...

UNNH...

GNNH...

UNH...

UUH...

UNNH...

BUN (BOMP)

BUN

SHUBA (ZOOM)

I'M SORRY, I'M SORRY!! PLEASE LET ME GO!!!

AAAAAAAH!!

DAMMIT! I ACTUALLY PLEADED FOR MY LIFE BACK THERE...!!!

WHAT THE HELL WAS THAT!!?

AH...

UWAAH !!!

WAIT A SEC... WHERE'S KIDO?

THEY CALLED THIS PLACE THE "DOLL HOUSE"...

I DON'T KNOW WHY THEY NEED COFFINS IN HERE TOO...

HAUNTED GROTESQUE DOLLHOUSE

COFFINS ...?

BUT WE'RE STILL PEEING OUR PANTS IN HERE ANYWAY...

HMM?

AND THE HANDS POPPING OUT OF THE WALLS? EVEN MORE OFF-THEME.

BUT THE ZOMBIES DIDN'T MAKE MUCH SENSE EITHER.

...THERE.

ZA
(ZWOOP)

SEE?

MOMO'S HIDING BEHIND THERE.

OH... IT'S JUST KISARAGI...!

TH—

TH—

THERE WHAT IS!? WHAT!!?

NOTHING! NO GHOSTS! OKAY!!?

SUTA (STRIDE)

SUTA

SUTA

WELL, GOOD THING WE FOUND HER...THANKS FOR THE HELP, SHINTARO.

OH YEAH, PLAY IT ALL COOL NOW......

KISA-RAGI!!

IT'S ME!

SORRY I LEFT YOU BEHIND.

LET'S GET OUT OF...

PRETTY VERSATILE ABILITY SHE'S GOT...

WOULD MAKE IT PRETTY EASY TO SNEAK INTO A PUBLIC BATH- HOUSE.

OKAY, I MADE IT SO THAT JUST KISARAGI'S INVISIBLE.

YOU AND I NEED TO KEEP GOING, SHINTARO.

SUU CVWEEEND

ZY

ZA CZWISH

AH!

I'VE FELT IT EVER SINCE I RAN INTO MOMO... WHAT IS IT...?

HUH...?

SOME- THING DOESN'T FEEL QUITE RIGHT...

AFTER ENE RODE THE ROLLER COASTER... WHERE'D SHE GO AFTER THAT?

HUH?

HM? WHAT'S UP, SHIN-TARO?

LET'S GET GOING.

HEY... KIDO?

SHE LEFT RIGHT AFTERWARD. SHE SAID SHE'D BE FOLLOWING YOU...?

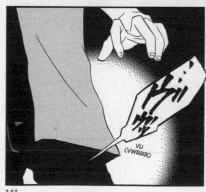

VU
(VWRRR)

"AAAAGH!!
My sweat-
shiiirt!!"

AAAGH!!!
LOOK,
STOP IT!!
STOP
PLAYING
THAT
BACK!!

"Oh man,
I don't
feel too
good...
Urk...
urgghk..."

AHH
HA
HA
HA!!!

IRA
IRA
(IRK)
IRA

"AAAAAAH!!
I'm sorry,
I'm sorry!!
Please let
me go!!!"

DUDE...

IRA
IRA

BACHI
(TING)

DID YOU HAVE FUN TODAY!?

...WELL...

WE STILL HAVE A LOT OF PLACES TO VISIT!

YEAH! BUT YOU KNOW... I HAVEN'T HAD A CHANCE TO PLAY AROUND AT ALL TODAY!

HUUUH!?

OH NO, NO NEED TO THANK ME!

OH NO?

THANKS A BUNCH.

THANKS TO YOU, IT WAS THE WORST DAY OF MY LIFE.

GICHI
(SQUEEZE)

HOW ABOUT THAT SHOOTING GAME, MASTER!?

THE ONE WHERE YOU SIT ON A STOOL AND BLAST AWAY AT ALIENS!!

DAMMIT... SHE NEVER GETS ENOUGH OF THIS.

SIGH...

OH!

HOW DO YOU EVEN KNOW THAT?

HAVE WE EVER PLAYED A SHOOTER TOGETHER?

YOU'RE REALLY GOOD AT SHOOTERS AND STUFF, RIGHT, MASTER?

HUH?

HEH...

I KNOW I'VE ASKED YOU THIS BEFORE...

...BUT... I MEAN, SERIOUSLY...

HEY... ENE?

...WHERE ON EARTH DID YOU COME FROM......?

...WELL, MASTER...

...THAT'S, YOU KNOW...?

MANGA VOLUME 2!

THANK YOU VERY MUCH...!!

THIS WAS THE CASE WITH VOLUME 1 AS WELL, BUT I'M SO EMBARRASSED AT SOME OF THE

PAGES I'VE DRAWN THAT IT'S HARD FOR ME TO EVEN LOOK AT THEM. I WONDER WHEN I'LL

EVER GET USED TO IT. I'M ALWAYS THINKING ABOUT HOW I WANT TO GET BETTER, BUT

REGARDLESS, ALL THE FEEDBACK AND LETTERS I'M RECEIVING ARE REALLY CHARGING ME UP

WITH ENERGY! I CAN'T THANK ALL OF YOU ENOUGH!! THANK YOU VERY MUCH...I'LL KEEP

POURING EVERYTHING I'VE GOT INTO THIS! SO I DEFINITELY (!) HOPE YOU'LL GIVE VOLUME 3
A READ AS WELL!! IT'LL BE GREAT IF
WE GET TO MEET AGAIN!!

佐藤まひろ MAHIRO SATOU

I SOMETIMES USE MANGA STUDIO, BUT WHAT A LEARNING CURVE!
THAT AND TABLETS...I HAVE NO IDEA HOW SIDU-SAN, WANNYANPUU-SAN,
AND EVERYONE ELSE CAN DRAW SUCH BEAUTIFUL LINES ON THEM. ALSO,
I WONDER WHY LIL' SOCKEYE IS JUST A SLICE OF FISH.

Congrats on the release of manga volume 2!!

I wrote a comment at the end of Volume 1 as well, but I received feedback from a lot of people that my handwriting was messy. Sorry about that. I haven't fixed anything since. I'll keep trying, though, so forgive me in the meantime.

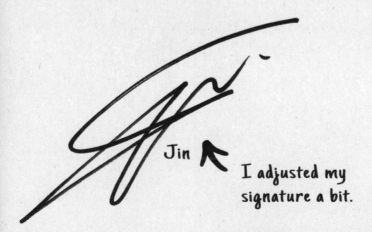

Jin

I adjusted my signature a bit.

VOLUME 2 IS OUT!! CONGRATULATIONS!

@Wannyanpuu-

First Volume 1, now Volume 2!! Sure goes by fast, doesn't it...!?
A ton of Mekakushi-dan members show up in this volume, so it
was a blast to read for me! Personally, I just can't get enough
of Seto...! And the Seto that Mahiro-san draws...Ohh! He's
soo, soooo handsome!! ('▽`*))) I love it!!
I wonder when Hibiya and Hiyori are gonna show up...!!
I can't wait to see what happens!!
And Takane-chan!! She's coming soon too!!
Please keep up the
good work!!

■TRANSLATION NOTES

Common Honorifics:
no honorific: Indicates familiarity or closeness; if used without permission or reason, addressing someone in this manner would constitute an insult.
-san: The Japanese equivalent of Mr./Mrs./Miss. If a situation calls for politeness, this is the fail-safe honorific.
-sama: Conveys great respect; may also indicate that the social status of the speaker is lower than that of the addressee.
-kun: Used most often when referring to boys, this indicates affection or familiarity. Occasionally used by older men among their peers, but it may also be used by anyone referring to a person of lower standing.
-chan: An affectionate honorific indicating familiarity used mostly in reference to girls; also used in reference to cute persons or animals of either gender.
-senpai: A suffix used to address upperclassmen or more experienced coworkers.
-sensei: A respectful term for teachers, artists, or high-level professionals.
-oniisan, onii-san, etc.: Terms used to address an elder brother or brother-like figure.
-oneesan, onee-san, etc.: Terms used to address an elder sister or sister-like figure.

Chapter Titles:
Each chapter title, as well as the title of this manga, refers to a specific musical composition from JIN (Shizen no Teki-P).

Kagerou means "mirage" or "heat haze." Jinzou means "artificial" or "man-made." Kisaragi is a poetic term for the second lunar month, but it can also be a surname. Finally, a mekakushi is a blindfold, thus Mekakushi-dan could be translated as "Blindfold Gang."

KAGEROU DAZE 02

MAHIRO SATOU
Original Story: JIN (SHIZEN NO TEKI-P)
Character Design: SIDU, WANNYANPUU-

Translation: Kevin Gifford • Lettering: Abigail Blackman

Kagerou Daze
© Mahiro Satou 2012-2015
© KAGEROU PROJECT / 1st PLACE 2012-2015
Edited by MEDIA FACTORY
First published in Japan in 2013 by KADOKAWA CORPORATION.
English translation rights reserved by HACHETTE BOOK GROUP, INC.
under the license from KADOKAWA CORPORATION, Tokyo
through TUTTLE-MORI AGENCY, Inc., Tokyo.

Translation © 2015 by Hachette Book Group, Inc.

Yen Press
Hachette Book Group
1290 Avenue of the Americas
New York, NY 10104

www.HachetteBookGroup.com
www.YenPress.com

Yen Press is an imprint of Hachette Book Group, Inc.
The Yen Press name and logo are trademarks of Hachette Book Group, Inc.

The publisher is not responsible for websites (or their content) that are not owned by the publisher.

First Yen Press Edition: July 2015

ISBN: 978-0-316-34619-1

10 9 8 7 6 5 4 3 2 1

BVG

Printed in the United States of America